My
Rainbow
Bible

God's world

Long ago, at the beginning of time,
God made light in the darkness.
God made mountains covered with snow
and deep lakes of cool water.

He filled the land with leafy trees
and made plants with juicy fruits.

God made the sunshine and the
moon and the stars.

God made night and day,
spring and summer,
autumn and winter.

God filled the water with fishes and the skies with colourful, chattering birds.

God made animals with long tails, big ears, funny noses and soft fur. And God made people to be his friends.

Noah's ark

God told Noah that there was going to be a flood that would cover the world.

'Build a big, big boat called an ark,' said God.

Noah took his family and all the animals inside and then the rain began to fall. It rained for forty days and forty nights.

Finally the rain stopped. Slowly the water went down. Noah waited until God told him to open the door and all the animals ran free. Noah thanked God for keeping them all safe.

Then God sent a beautiful rainbow.

Joseph's big brothers

Joseph's mother died when he was little, but Joseph's dad loved him very much. Joseph had lots of big brothers – they didn't like him at all!

8

But God loved Joseph and looked after him.
God made sure that, when there wasn't enough food
to eat where they lived, Joseph was in Egypt to help his
family and all God's people.

Moses, the baby in the basket

Moses' mother hid him from the cruel King in Egypt. God made sure he was kept safe. When the princess found Moses, she looked after him.

10

God had a job for Moses.
When he was grown up, he led God's
people out of slavery in Egypt to a
land where they could worship
and love God in freedom.

David and Goliath

David wasn't as big and strong as his brothers. He wasn't as big and strong as King Saul. He wasn't as big and strong as the giant, Goliath!

The soldiers were afraid and King Saul was afraid. But David knew that God was big and strong and not afraid at all.

David trusted God. He fought Goliath
– and God helped David to win the battle!

Jonah and the big fish

God sent Jonah to tell people
that they must stop doing bad things. But Jonah
didn't want to. He got on a ship – and tried to
hide from God.

A big fish came to swallow Jonah. Then Jonah told God he was sorry he had run away. The big fish spat Jonah out. This time Jonah took God's message to the people. When they were sorry, God showed how much he loved them and he forgave them.

Daniel and the lions

Daniel was thrown into a den of lions!

Daniel lived in a country where he was
not allowed to pray. But Daniel loved God
and he wanted to pray to him.

And because God loved Daniel he kept
him safe. The lions did not eat him!

Baby Jesus

Mary had a very special baby, Jesus.
He was the Son of God.

Mary made a bed for Jesus in a manger in Bethlehem because there was no room for them in the inn.

Angels announced the good news to shepherds, who were on a hillside looking after their sheep.

Later, wise men saw a new star in the sky and came to worship Jesus, the baby King.

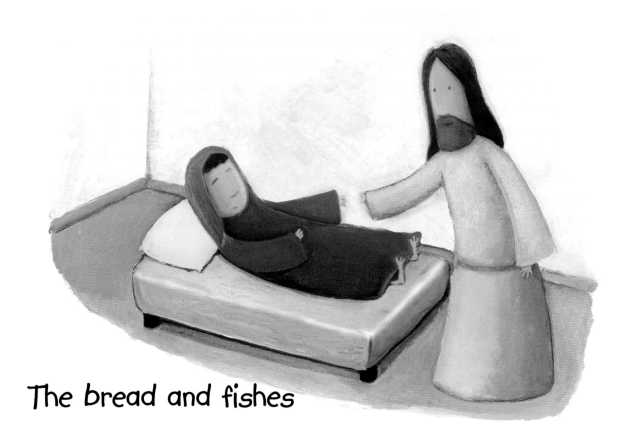

The bread and fishes

When he was grown up, Jesus showed people how much
God loved them.

He looked after people who were ill
or sad or lonely.

One day Jesus gave food to thousands of people who were hungry. He shared out five loaves and two little fish – and everyone had enough to eat!

Jesus calms a storm

Once there was a storm on the sea. The disciples' little boat was rocked up and down and they were very afraid.

Jesus had fallen asleep. But when he woke up, he told the wind to stop blowing and the waves to stop splashing. And the sea was calm again.

Jesus heals a blind man

Bartimaeus sat by the roadside day after day
and begged for money. He was blind and could
not see.

When Jesus came by, Bartimaeus called to him for help. And Jesus listened. He made Bartimaeus see – and Bartimaeus was so happy, he became Jesus' friend.

Soldiers in the garden

Peter tried to stay awake while Jesus prayed in the garden. Then he watched as soldiers came and took his friend Jesus away.

26

Peter had seen the kind things Jesus did. Peter heard
Jesus tell everyone that God loved them.
Now he watched as cruel men
made Jesus carry his cross
through the streets.

Easter morning

Mary cried as Jesus died on a cross. She followed when they buried his body in a tomb.

Two days later, she laughed and cried at the same time! The stone was rolled away.

The tomb was empty!

God had brought Jesus back from the dead and now he was alive again, talking to her in the garden! And Jesus would never die again.

First edition 2018

Copyright © 2018 Anno Domini Publishing
www.ad-publishing.com
Text copyright © 2018 Bethan James
Illustrations copyright © 2007 Yorgos Sgouros

Publishing Director: Annette Reynolds
Art Director: Gerald Rogers
Pre-production Manager: Doug Hewitt

Published 2018 by Authentic Media Ltd,
PO Box 6326, Bletchley, Milton Keynes, MKI 9GG
Conforms to EN71 and AS/NZS ISO 8124

Printed and bound in Malaysia